SPEAKING IN CLOTH

Ann Johnston and Jeannette DeNicolis Meyer

with Cynthia Corbin, Quinn Zander Corum, Nancy Erickson, Trisha Hassler

6 *Quilters*
6 *Voices*

Ann Johnston, Publisher
Lake Oswego, Oregon
USA

acknowledgements

Jim Johnston is just happy Ann can get back to her ukulele.

Bill Meyer, patient as usual, manned the computer and reminded Jeannette to breathe.

Ann Marra's design talent is evident on every page of this book.

MJ Koreiva's ongoing support of the art quilt provided a museum space that allowed us to think big. We're still waiting for our tango lessons.

Cynthia Corbin, Nancy Erickson, Quinn Zander Corum, and Trisha Hassler are artists to applaud, both for their artwork and for their ability to meet deadlines.

Speaking in Cloth: 6 Quilters, 6 Voices

Library of Congress Control Number: 2006905307
ISBN 13: 978-0-9656776-2-2
ISBN 10: 0-9656776-2-1

Published by Ann Johnston, P.O. Box 944, Lake Oswego, OR 97034 USA
www.annjohnston.net

Designer: Ann Marra
Artwork Photography:
  Bill Bachhuber: Ann Johnston, Jeannette DeNicolis Meyer, Quinn Zander Corum
  Ken Wagner: Cynthia Corbin
  Nancy Erickson: Nancy Erickson
  Nate Hassler: Trisha Hassler
Color Production: Jerry Sayer
Printed in Hong Kong

OREGON ARTS
COMMISSION

NATIONAL
ENDOWMENT
FOR THE ARTS

This project is supported in part by an award from the Oregon Arts Commission and the National Endowment for the Arts.

table of contents

foreword

In this first decade of the 21st Century, Coos Art Museum has presented three biennial museum-wide art quilt exhibitions consisting of solo shows, juried group competitions, and internationally curated traveling exhibits. The Museum has seen first hand how enthusiastically a broad audience embraces the art quilt medium. It has become a form of artistic expression for contemporary artists to use thread and fabric as a painter uses oil and acrylic. The manipulability of its core material, fabric—dyed, painted, cut, torn, pieced, appliquéd, fused, glued, beaded, embroidered, layered, and finally, stitched—allows the artists to create original color, form, and imagery within this medium. The textural qualities that are created by the stitching give artists additional tools that allow for a wide array of possible expressions. The artists' use of texture helps to reveal the hand of the maker, connecting viewers to their work in a relationship unique to fiber.

Speaking in Cloth: 6 Quilters, 6 Voices brings together new works by six of the Pacific Northwest's most dynamic and creative artists working today in the art quilt medium. Co-curators Ann Johnston and Jeannette DeNicolis Meyer together bring fifty years of experience with textile art to the production of the exhibit and its accompanying catalog.

In this exhibit, Johnston and Meyer, with Cynthia Corbin, Quinn Zander Corum, Nancy Erickson and Trisha Hassler, are presenting a body of work that will set the tone for the early 21st Century art quilt medium in our region. These are fully realized works of art that draw you near, beckoning you to look closely and then asking you to step back and think—and join the conversation.

Coos Art Museum continues its support of regional contemporary artists by providing an art museum setting for this important form of art. As the third oldest art museum in Oregon, Coos Art Museum's mission is to present works by contemporary artists of our region to help ensure that they become a part of our future cultural heritage.

MJ Koreiva, Executive Director
Coos Art Museum

2006

Coos
Art Museum

introduction

The vocabulary of quilts is an expansive addition to the language of art, because of its extensive use of layer and texture. The artists we invited to exhibit in *Speaking in Cloth: 6 Quilters, 6 Voices* employ this vocabulary to speak in their own voices. They use cloth, batting, and thread to tell their stories and record their explorations. The far-ranging experiments of these six artists have resulted in an exhibit that demonstrates the possibilities of art quilts.

As exhibit producers our goal was to invite an art-viewing audience fluent in the language of other visual arts to join a conversation with us as we speak in fabric and stitches. *Speaking in Cloth: 6 Quilters, 6 Voices* begins an ongoing dialogue between those of us who choose fiber to make art and viewers who recognize that the quilt is an expressive and arresting art form.

Thanks to MJ Koreiva's invitation to produce an exhibit of six Northwest quilt artists, we are able to present the work of Nancy Erickson, Trisha Hassler, Cynthia Corbin, and Quinn Zander Corum, along with our own, in the spacious galleries of the Coos Art Museum. Nancy Erickson is a Montana artist whose figurative painted quilts depict interactions between animals and humans that beg the viewer to supply a narrative. Washington artist Cynthia Corbin's figures appear out of and return to heavily patterned grounds, which have been dyed, printed, pieced, and stitched into abstraction. Oregonian Quinn Zander Corum alters and combines perspectives in her hand appliquéd and embroidered work, blurring the line between the microscopic and the cosmic. Trisha Hassler,

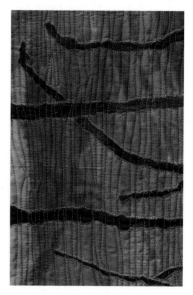

another Oregonian, also explores opposites in her mixed media pieces juxtaposing hard and soft, metal and fiber, wire and thread. Ann Johnston employs her expertise with dyes and hand and machine stitching to produce a body of work remarkable for its visual variety and bold gestures. Jeannette DeNicolis Meyer's daily push/pull between meditation and movement, intuition and planning, is recorded in the surfaces of her quilts. Although visually diverse, the work of these six artists shares a belief that thematic concerns can be addressed with layers and texture, needle and thread.

This book, which accompanies the exhibit and extends the conversation between the artists and the viewer, is structured around questions that we are often asked and that we often ask each other.

> Why do you choose the language of fiber and thread to make your art?
> Do you find yourself working with recurring themes over time?
> Is there a visual voice that identifies your work?
> What are your working processes?
> What are the challenges and joys of making your art?
> Does it matter if the quilt communicates a specific message to your viewers?

In these chapters, we begin to answer these questions with both our words and our artwork. We look forward to continuing the conversation.

Ann Johnston and Jeannette DeNicolis Meyer, Producers

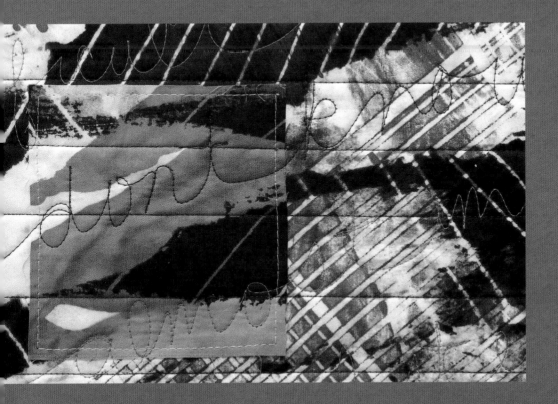

language

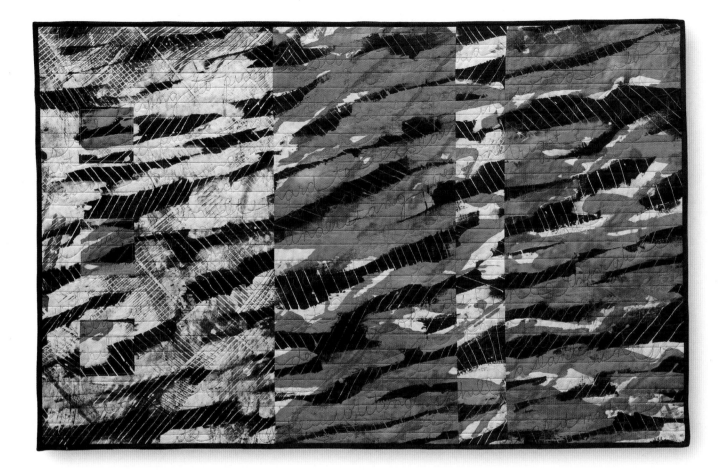

Ann: I chose cloth and stitches as a means of expression because they were accessible and familiar. More than 30 years later, I still find the desire to manipulate cloth an irresistible force. I start with white fabric, create my colors and make my marks, limited only by what I can imagine and what skill I can develop. I am fascinated with the potential of combining my own dyed cloth with a variety of techniques—piecing, appliqué, embroidery, quilting. The textures my stitches create are integral to the content and the composition of my quilts.

Ann Johnston, *Writing Uphill*, 2006, 34″ x 54″

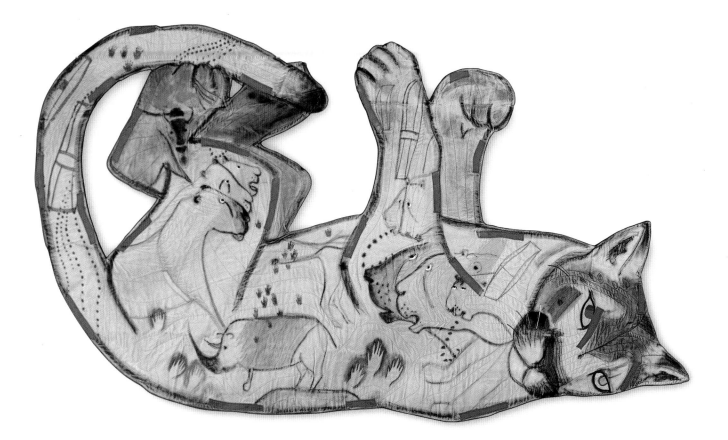

Nancy: The advantage of working in fabric is that it is so versatile. One can print on, paint on, draw on (I inadvertently walked on *Easter Cougar* with my shoes covered with paint, and it was fine), sew through and stuff fabric. I've done all of those with my works over the years, and intersplicing fabric work with drawing and painting helps to work out new ideas. Also, one can work large in fabric, easily, and I do like to work large.

Nancy Erickson, *Easter Cougar*, 2001, 46″ x 72″

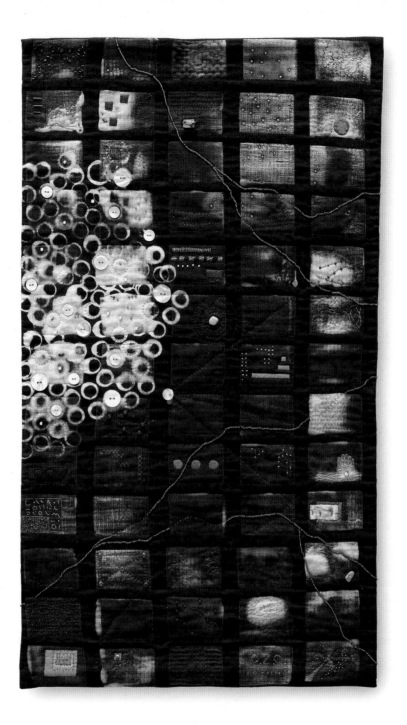

Quinn: It was a natural progression for me to do art/in cloth/with stitching. I feel like I've always sewn, and I'm sure my family would agree that I've always done things a little differently.

I love that I work in fabric—an everyday item, familiar to everyone—and that with the traditional techniques of sewing and quilting I create something that speaks an art-cloth language entirely different from the one familiar to most people.

Quinn Zander Corum, *Night Skies*, 2005, 34" x 19"

Jeannette: The way a quilt is constructed, layer after layer, over time, is a lot like how life is lived. The choice of such a time-consuming medium may seem perverse, but I like the time spent with each layer, both with my head and with my hands. It gives me a chance to imagine the next part of the conversation, the next layer of color, stitch and meaning. Ever since I can remember I've drawn and colored when given a spare minute and a blank surface, and I'm still doing that now, except with fabric and dye and thread.

Jeannette DeNicolis Meyer, *Contrapuntal*, 2005, 33″ x 72″

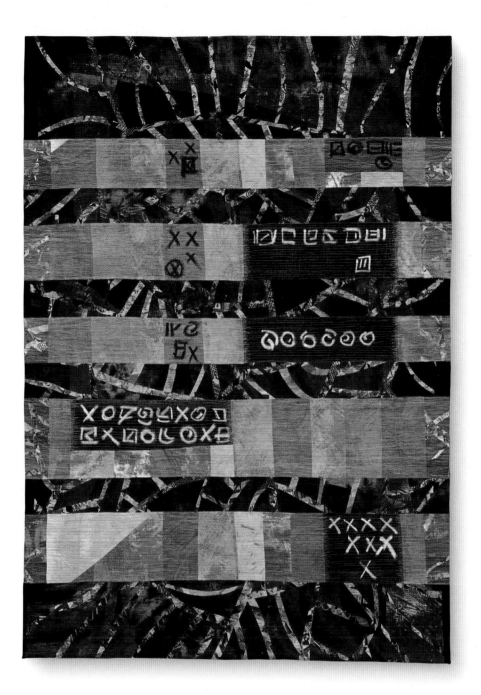

Cynthia: My grandmother made ugly quilts—made to be used hard. Her tops were crazy patched clothing remnants, tied over old wool blankets. I slept pinned down under the weight of those quilts, touching the fabrics, hearing stories of my Colorado prairie family.

Grandma's quilts were abstract by necessity—she used every bit of what she had. I *choose* abstract form and variation in textures and pattern. I find myself "writing" into the fabrics and stitches a measure of experience, an accounting of my own time.

Cynthia Corbin, *Adds Up (Painted Pieces Series)*, 2005, 77″ x 54″

Trisha: I love the tactile sensation of textiles. I purchase clothing, furniture and dish towels by how they feel first. Texture, drape, and color all inspire me. I'm the one in a museum or quilt show the docents watch because I want to touch everything. Fabric has recorded the history of the world through stitch, often crossing language barriers. The needle arts traditions run deep in my heritage and I have done some sort of stitching since childhood. I've tried other mediums but everything resembled a quilt, either in pattern or construction. Finally, I got it. This is my medium of expression. I do fiber.

Trisha Hassler, *Working With My Ancestral Baggage*, 2006, 19″ x 16″

theme

Cynthia: I'm trying to understand something—about the fabric, the marks, the shapes, the colors—and about what they come to mean. I want to understand my own choices, my own preferences, and what *they* come to mean. So I try lots of things. I look for the unfamiliar, and explore ways of varying a shape, or a line, or the texture—just to see what it does, to find what it suggests to me, and what it ultimately comes to say.

I'm thinking, always, about communication.

Cynthia Corbin, *Journey Man (The Crowd Series)*, 2003, 74″ x 54″

Quinn: I've moved around a lot regarding subjects in my work, but I think what is most important to me is interpreting an idea in a new and different way.

I've been working on the *Earth Forms* series for several years. Some are landforms seen from high above the Earth, others are small maps, some are close-ups or cross sections of geographic or structural elements, and some combine all of these and more. What I want to end up with is the suggestion of a time and place, but more importantly, with a *feeling* for such a place.

Quinn Zander Corum, *EARTH FORMS: The Pond,* 2006, 26″ x 19″

Trisha: The paradox of balance is a recurring theme for me, in my art, as well as in my life. I seem to be always on one side or the other of the illusive "centered" state, although I do have more success finding that balance in my artwork. I am drawn to imagery that speaks about the compromises of male/female, hard/soft, and old/new. The place where each works together, complementing each other, is more illusive in reality. I am always struck by the irony of finding balance in my art while continuing to obsess about details in my everyday world.

　　　　　　　　　　　Trisha Hassler, *Finally*, 2005, 22″ x 16″

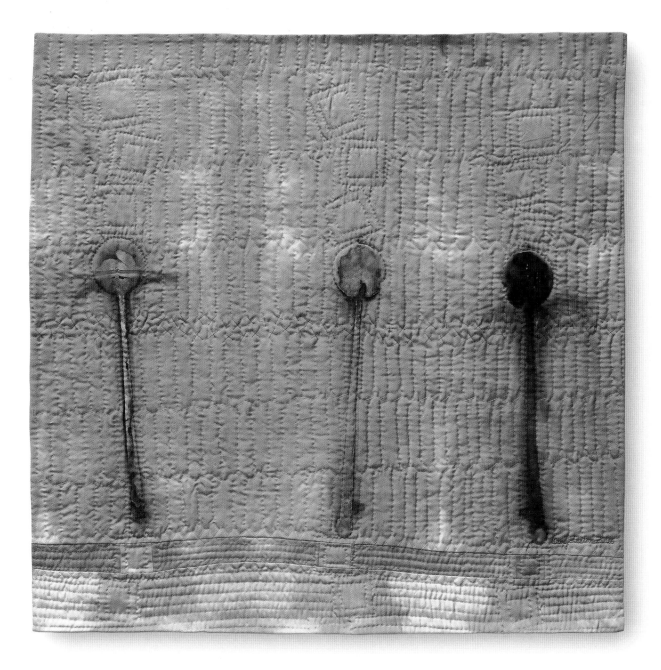

Ann: I am extremely interested in how an idea becomes a physical form. The only way I can start to understand this is in my own work, observing my own thought processes that take me to the end result. So while many of my quilts directly treat a theme—balance versus chaos, for example—they are also indirectly about how the ideas develop within the decisions I make. As many ways as I have tried to set an idea in cloth, I keep finding even more ways to approach the same idea in yet another quilt. I think that all my quilts together are about this exploration.

Ann Johnston, *Balance #27: Three*, 2006, 31″ × 32″

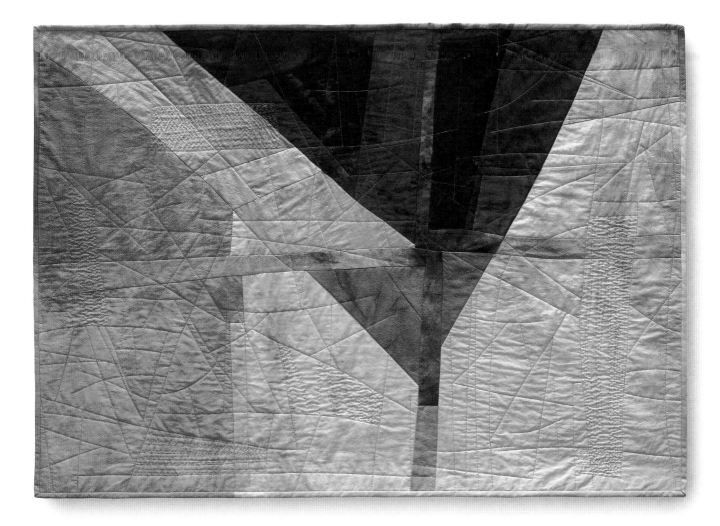

Jeannette: All of my work explores relationships, how matter from atoms to humans are related and entwined and yet ultimately alone in this shifting cosmic composition. I strive to translate this fascination with how we exist as individuals and as part of a whole to the visual organization of my quilts. I try to make areas on the quilt's surface relate to each other in a way that's personal to me but leaves meditative spaces open to viewers to walk into and figure out their own relationship to it.

Jeannette DeNicolis Meyer, *Flight Plan*, 2006, 32″ x 46″

Nancy: In my work, objects, landscapes, humans and other animals interact in quilted and painted fabrics. Sometimes the pieces are more abstract, as in the cave drawings on the forms, but the idea usually starts with these elements.

Nancy Erickson, *Hall of Memory #8: The Ecstasy Which Occurs*
Upon Discovering Cave Bear Ancestors, 1998, 59″ x 60″

voice

Trisha: Weathered steel is my current artistic trademark. Attention to detail and an intimacy created by detailed stitching rewards the viewer who takes a closer look. Amish and pioneer patterns are strong influences in my work. The palette I have been working with recently is helping me find answers to the challenge of balance. My pieces are mine because they express my hopes and emotions. I resist the temptation to rework, redesign or clean up the ideas too much. The artwork is recognizable as a body of work because they all come from the same place in me.

Trisha Hassler, *Can't Live With 'Em, Can't Shoot 'Em*, 2006, 18″ x 38″

Quinn: I think people recognize my work for its unusual imagery, as well as for its heavily embroidered and hand appliquéd details. Because I often work with images seen from unique perspectives, much of my work appears abstract. My colors don't have to accurately reflect what is represented. Still, appliqué and embroidery form the bones of my work; they help build the imagery, provide the embellishing lines, and often serve as the quilting to hold the work together.

Quinn Zander Corum, *The Back Forty #31*, 2006, 8″ x 5″

Jeannette: The deliberate way I work and my use of color, line and space define my quilts. I strive to make the design and construction decisions seem like inevitable answers to the questions I'm asking myself as I begin. I tend to use a working vocabulary of complex colors without much value shift, rectangles divided and redivided with angles and arcs, pieced and quilted lines that flow and intertwine, moons that wax and wane.

Jeannette DeNicolis Meyer, *Conundrum*, 2006, 24″ x 22″

Nancy: Animals are interacting with humans in some form in almost all my art. Some visual narratives are humorous, as with *By the Light of the Volcano: Hand Shadows #3* where humans and bears attempt hand shadows on a sheet with volcanic eruptions behind.

Many of the works are painted as paintings, reflecting my degrees in painting and drawing, but all are added to and quilted by machine. Color is really the reason I went into art, and it is still very important to me.

Nancy Erickson, *By the Light of the Volcano: Hand Shadows #3*, 1995, 71″ x 63″

Cynthia: I tend to quilt the heck out of my work. I love line upon line of stitching, the push and shove of pattern against pattern, and oddball colors.

Circles and squares intrigue me as ambiguous symbols. They infuse an ongoing conversation with myself. Whether painted, pieced or stitched, I am counting, organizing, measuring, adding up. I'm thinking about aging, time passing, marks of measuring time and experiences, and the evidence left behind by erosion, fading, or wearing away.

Cynthia Corbin, *Binary (The Crowd Series)*, 2003, 76″ x 57″

Ann: Over the last 25 years of dyeing all the cloth for my quilts, I have developed a fairly fearless approach to color, pattern and line. Each piece of cloth contains the moment I made it. I continuously find within my fabric ways to draw together my diverse experiences and interests, and I think my quilts show my excitement in discovery. My fabric demands stitches on it and I never hide them, but rather use them to create a textural composition overlaying the colors and pieces below, always in an attempt to add meaning.

Ann Johnston, *Earth Lines*, 2006, 52″ x 35″

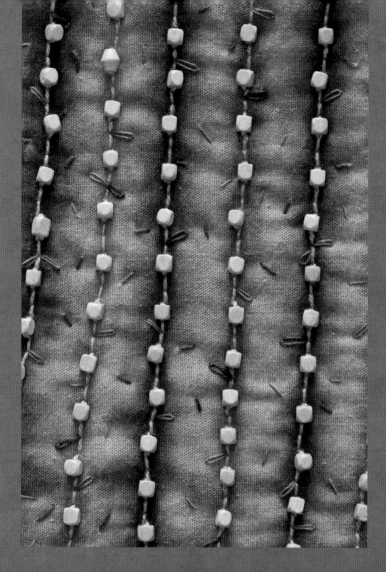

process

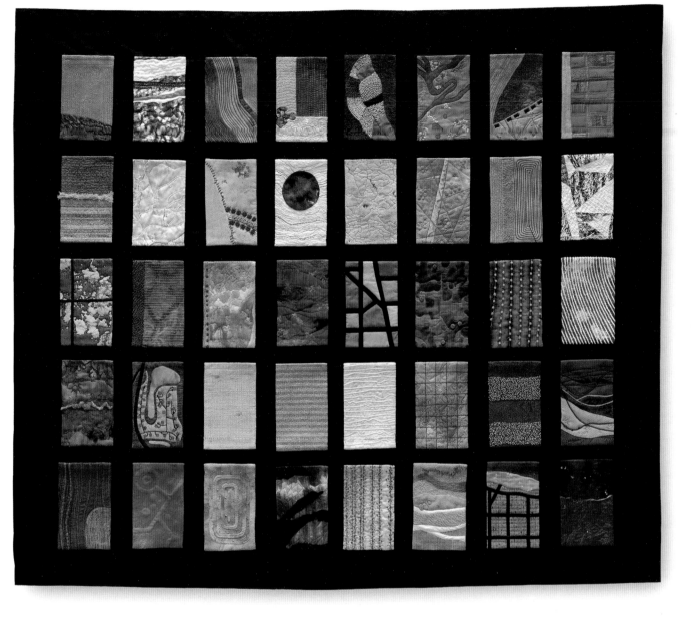

Quinn: Ideas for *The Back Forty* came from several directions at the same time: growing up on a farm, recalling the forty acres that were farthest from the homestead and not seen from the road, the marginal land, the land getting the least attention, or perhaps the most-treasured acreage. Imagine the possibilities! Some of the individual pieces were sketched first; some evolved as I sewed and saw the place. Ideas changed and all sorts of personal symbolism developed with each of the forty and with the piece as a whole.

Quinn Zander Corum, *The Back Forty*, 2006, 54″ x 62″

Jeannette: After I figure out what idea I'm working on—which takes me longer than anything else—making quilts is a dance, with forward and backward motion and long rests as the intent and structure of the dance become evident. Sometimes I start with sketches that serve as visual memos as I start moving fabric around. Occasionally a quilt emerges with the fabric from the dye bath. However the dance begins, one step determines the next, each layer informs the next.

Jeannette DeNicolis Meyer, *Dancing in the Dark*, 2006, 47″ x 64″

Nancy: Often I start with a specific event. The cave series came about from reading books and from seeing new collections of the French cave drawings. The event then takes the form of a story, which leads to thinking about the players in the drama, and a simple drawing. The drawing is placed on fabric directly, or is projected onto paper or plastic, and then transferred to the fabric for a whole cloth quilt. The piece is painted, then elements added. I follow the same procedure on the figure works, which are taken from models in our drawing group.

Nancy Erickson, *Felis Forever (3)*, 2000, 74″ x 47″

Trisha: I carry a sketchbook and am always ready to scribble a pattern, or some germ of an idea for reference. When I have studio time, it may be a sketch, a piece of fabric or chunk of steel that gets me going. I often write the working title on a post-it attached to the table where I sew, editing the words while the work evolves. As I work improvisationally, the piece develops and becomes more complex. The final artwork is a visual record of my creative journey expressing the evolution of my thoughts.

Trisha Hassler, *Explosion of the Soul*, 2006, 18″ x 33″

Cynthia: I want to squeeze every bit of information I can out of an idea. What will happen? I am willing to screw it up in order to find out—going "too far" to see how far is "too far." I am also willing to go really quiet to see when it wilts. I work to find and explore the limits, playing with elements of accident, scrambling up bits of fabric, color, and texture—looking for evocative forms and relationships.

Making a mistake or wrong turn is useful. I can see. I can learn.

Cynthia Corbin, *Sums (Painted Pieces Series)*, 2006, 60″ x 31″

Ann: I have a growing store of ideas and I make them into quilts as I find ways. The fabrics I have already dyed sometimes prompt an idea, because they are already gestures of my own. I audition the fabrics, make thumbnail sketches, and choose techniques that not only enhance the concept, but also are a pleasure to perform. Building the quilt is like following a thread of visual thought through a maze of possibilities, except that I am starting at the middle point. My exploration could take me many places.

Ann Johnston, *Baseline*, 2005, 20″ x 38″

challenge

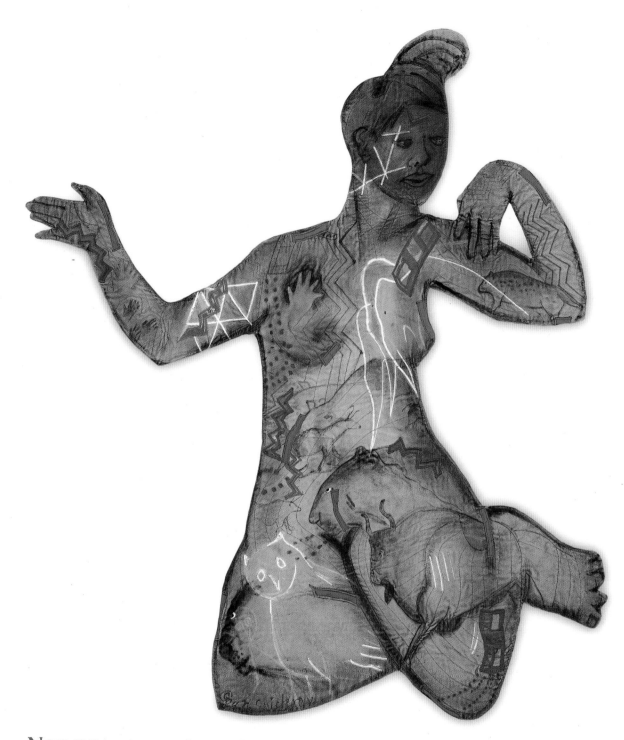

Nancy: Finding an idea worth pursuing is sometimes hard. Then, when there are a zillion ideas, just choosing the best one and making it work is sometimes difficult. It is rare for me that a piece just works smoothly all the way through. It's lurch after lurch usually, and when the art does move quickly, the piece is sometimes just boring.

Nancy Erickson, *Storyteller*, 2004, 60″ x 50″

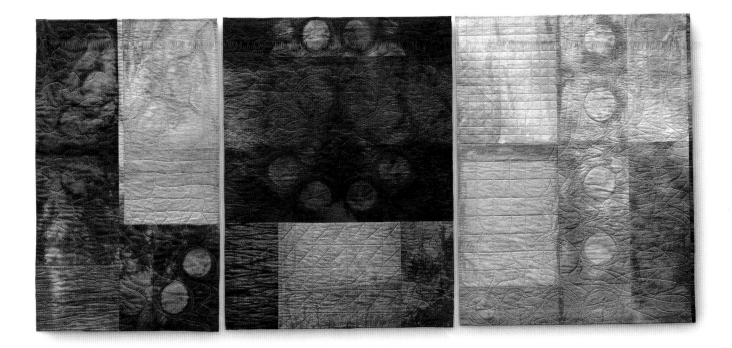

Jeannette: The hardest part of making art for me is starting. Once I clear the room of critics and exhaust all avenues of procrastination and finally begin, I love how the slow process of working layer by layer involves a rhythm of cerebration and handwork. Manipulating the materials engages my hands and lets my mind roam, clearing my brain of chatter. I love those moments, when all, or maybe most, is revealed, the design decisions click into place and life is good. Until I finish, and am faced with a blank wall again.

Jeannette DeNicolis Meyer, *Winter Diary*, 2006, 37″ x 80″

Cynthia: The hardest thing is working through my own uncertainty. It can grab me at any time. You know that voice mumbling through your thoughts? Intruding with, "WHY did you do that?" or "THAT didn't work, did it?" I often shut it up by listening to old movies as I sew—especially old B-westerns. I don't know, but there is just something about gunfire and the pounding of horses' hooves that works for me. Maybe it's the Zen of the Western.

The works in the *Painted Pieces Series* are my most recent adventures with horses' hooves and gunfire.

Cynthia Corbin, *Blanket (Painted Pieces Series)*, 2005, 60″ x 56″

Quinn: Making the quilts is always a pleasure, even when there are problems or frustrations—it would be boring if there were no challenges. I feel really fortunate to be able to work at something I enjoy so much.

I love working with fabric and sewing. I love to experiment and take chances in both imagery and technique. I'm usually eager to get on to the next piece and, in fact, I often have several pieces in various stages of design and construction going at once.

Quinn Zander Corum, *EARTH FORMS: Dry Arroyo*, 2000, 30″ x 41″

Trisha: The biggest difficulty for me is cutting into a piece of hand-dyed fabric that seems to have so many possibilities. By cutting, I choose one direction and other ideas have to be let go. The easiest and most enjoyable part of my process is the stitching. By the time I get to that part, the visual is complete in my head, the steel is cut, sealed, and ready, and ideas are flowing freely. The work still shifts and changes during this part of the process, but without blocks or technical challenges. I can truly get lost in French knots.

Trisha Hassler, *Symmetry is Highly Overrated*, 2006, 37″ x 33″

Ann: What is exciting and fun is having a solution appear when I had no conscious idea what it would be before I started. I work hard to be able to see the design possibilities all around me and I also work hard at keeping many pathways open at each turn. What is difficult is telling people who ask what my work means. A lot of my ideas are connected to words, but spelling out the ideas is not fun or easy. I would rather let the quilt speak for me with its visual language.

Ann Johnston, *Fallen*, 2006, 51″ x 65″

message

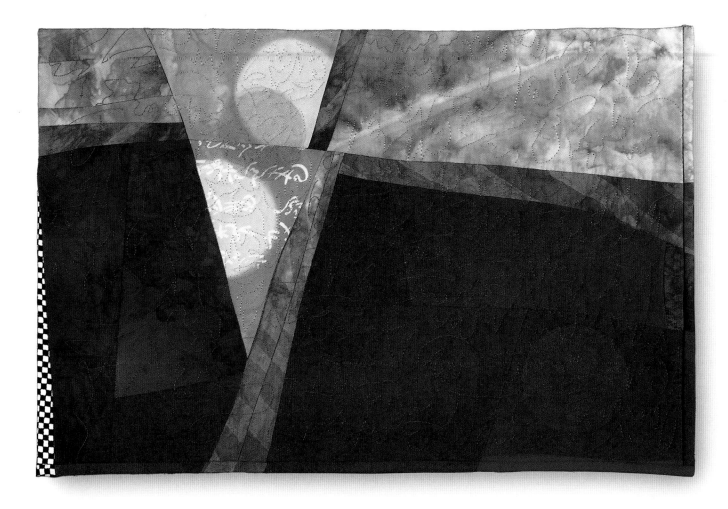

Jeannette: It matters more to me that viewers sense an authentic voice than a specific meaning in my work. Maybe it all boils down to making art to leave my hand on the cave wall, to say, "I was here, this is what it was like for me." My quilts are pretty quiet, and I think that's because I want people to be able to stop in front of them and hear themselves think about what it's like for *them* while they're wandering through my fields of line and color.

Jeannette DeNicolis Meyer, *Night Words*, 2003, 15″ x 22″

Nancy: It is fine if people just relate to the design elements of a work. As in most art, though, many levels of complexity can be found. In both *Hall of Memory #8* and *Hall of Memory #9* the cave bears' re-visiting their past after humans, presumably, are gone, seems to refer to the element of extinction. The women sit with their ancient fires talking and contemplating the flames, a universal experience.

I hope that the title of a work is helpful, but looking at the art work itself should suggest its meaning.

Nancy Erickson, *Hall of Memory #9; A Room of One's Own,* 1998, 60˝ x 71˝

Ann: My quilts come out of the accidental meetings of forms and colors and my pursuit of tying together meanings for myself. I want viewers of my quilts to be free to respond and absorb according to their own worlds. Some will follow the choices I have made and analyze how I work, and others will relate to its overall visual impact, and then as they get closer, to the details. When I am following the thread of thought, making the quilt, it is my meaning, often an evolving meaning—when you are looking at it, it's yours.

Ann Johnston, *In the Rain of Chaos*, 2006, 26″ x 17″

Cynthia: I work to please myself during the building of a quilt—answering my own questions about the processes, materials, and effects I am using. I *do* think about and search for meaning in every quilt. I'm looking for something that makes sense of it for me. Somehow, and mysteriously, what I am thinking and questioning seeps into the stitches.

My titles suggest a place to start a conversation—one that is unique to each person looking at that quilt. My meaning is not the only meaning. I want to invite the viewer in.

Cynthia Corbin, *Stand Off (The Crowd Series)*, 2003, 76″ x 54″

Trisha: My titles have become an important part of each piece because I feel I am stitching my stories. The words are a starting point for the viewer to discover what the piece will say to them. People seem to appreciate the words as the beginning of a dialog, and have even made a final choice to own a piece based on its title. I don't include any additional information or analysis. If I wanted to be more explicit, I would have chosen to be a writer. But I didn't choose words, I chose fabric.

Trisha Hassler, *On the Street Where I Live*, 2006, 12″ x 34″

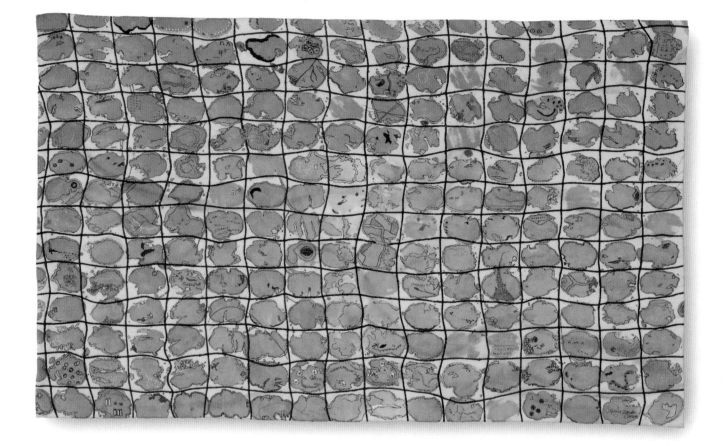

Quinn: I can't imagine a viewer getting exactly what I was thinking when I made a quilt. Each piece develops and changes for me as I work on it.

I like it best when someone glances up and notices one of my quilts and it makes them feel something and makes them curious. They come closer and then they are pulled into the work by surprises of detail that were unseen from a distance. They are intrigued and even more curious. Then the viewer has a relationship of their own with the work. That's exciting.

Quinn Zander Corum, *Navigating Life*, 2003, 27″ x 44″

Cynthia Corbin
www.cynthiacorbin.com

Cynthia sees her work as an eclectic personal expression in classical quilt form. Using a seat of the pants approach to quilt construction, she explores marking fabric with dye, paint and intensive machine quilting. Her work has been published and exhibited throughout the United States and Europe. She lectures and teaches nationally. As an artist, Cynthia has devoted herself to extensive study to deepen her understanding of the processes that drive her work. As a teacher, she encourages her students to search for uniqueness and authenticity in their own work. Cynthia lives and works in Woodinville, Washington.

Quinn Zander Corum
www.quinnzandercorum.com

To confuse things, Quinn's given name is Gwen. She grew up on a farm in Minnesota, raised chickens with the Peace Corps in India, earned a degree in cultural anthropology from Cal/Berkeley, and lived in Brazil where she learned to play tennis, one of her greatest pleasures. Quinn has worked with needle and thread since learning to hand embroider at age five, and has been exhibiting her art quilts since 1987. She makes her home with her husband Kenton and their two above-average sons in Portland, Oregon.

Nancy Erickson
www.nancyerickson.com

At the beginning of World War II Nancy's parents bought a fabulous cattle ranch (Mission Ranch) near Livingston, Montana, and set about changing their lives radically. As a child she spent hours wandering the mountains and foothills of the Absarokees. After the ranch, Nancy says she picked up an educated layer earning degrees in zoology, nutrition and finally an MA and an MFA in painting. She has lived with her husband Ron in the same mountain canyon near Missoula, Montana for 35 years, enjoying the company of cougars, bears, and deer.

Trisha Hassler
www.trishahassler.com

Since childhood, Trisha has stitched, cut and reassembled everything that would hold still. Along the way were baby quilts, clothing, dance costumes, scenery and even a sofa. She developed a fascination with construction techniques, improvisational quilting and alternative materials. The evolution of her artwork continued through experimentation and the discovery of metal. Trisha's artwork is exhibited in juried shows, galleries and museums across the country. As full-time stylist in her husband's photography studio, she works with fabric daily. Many ideas grow from their photo projects, and by the end of the day she's ready to stitch again.

Ann Johnston
www.annjohnston.net

First, Ann learned to sew, then she learned to dye fabric. In between, she earned a degree in Literature from Stanford University and a Masters in Geography at the University of Oregon. She taught new math in Lima, Peru, raised two sons in Oregon with her husband Jim, and started quilting. Ann's years of experimentation with dye and fabric have led to piles of quilts, worldwide travel, numerous group and solo exhibitions, and five books. Her collectors respect her viewpoint and her students admire her generosity and skill in teaching what she knows.

Jeannette DeNicolis Meyer
www.jdmeyer.com

Jeannette grew up in New York, where her parents kept her supplied with colored pencils and her uncle taught her to sew. Accompanying her eighth grade French class to Europe awakened a lifelong love of travel, a reverence for art museums, and an awe of all middle school teachers. She and her husband headed west after graduating from Cornell and, except for a brief move to New Zealand, raised their two sons in Oregon. Jeannette exhibits and conducts dye and design workshops internationally, teaches in the studio school of the Oregon College of Art and Craft, and hopes to make art until the light gives out.